PREFACE, BIOGRAPHY & COPYRIGHT

Of great significance to everyone interested in Native American Culture, this excellently researched and rendered book is designed to educate as well as entertain. It is filled with fun facts and ready-to-color symbols illustrated from ancient artifacts and designs of the American Indian Tribes of the South East Woodlands of North America. This book will intrigue and captivate people of all ages. An enjoyable collection of drawings and information it can also serve as an important classroom teaching aid.

Timothy P. Locklear II is a member of the Lumbee Tribe of North Carolina, and specializes in Native American graphic and jewelry design from Pembroke, NC. Two of his credits are designing the Lumbee Ring and Pinecone Patchwork Jewelry, which is a way to preserve key events, dates and symbols of Lumbee tribal history. He also designed the current University of North Carolina at Pembroke Logo. He currently serves as coordinator of Cyna's 3E a local non-profit with goals intended to Enhance, Educate and Empower the local Native American community. A graduate of Indiana Wesleyan University with a BA degree in Biblical Studies prompted the development of Serving People in Need (SPIN) Ministry that focuses on providing bible study and prayer in a number of local Nursing Care facilities. He is also a contributing writer to the Native Vision Magazine and board member of Cyna's Jewelers Inc.

Jamie K. Oxendine of the Lumbee Tribe of North Carolina, is a Native American Educator, Historian and Speaker. He has been an Adjunct Professor of Native American Studies at Bowling Green State University, Ohio State University, University of Toledo, Lourdes University, and has served as the Native American Liaison & Education Consultant for Ohio University. He has served on the Board of Trustees for the Ohio Humanities Council, Board of Trustees for the Fallen Timbers Battlefield Preservation Commission and Governor Appointee to the Ohio Historic Site Preservation Board. He has also sat on the ACCESS Grants Panel with the National Endowment For The Humanities.

ISBN: 978-0-692-11099-7
Library of Congress Control Number: 2018942859
Illustrations by Timothy P. Locklear II
Cover Illustration Copyright © 2018 by Timothy P. Locklear II
Writing Author by Jamie K. Oxendine

SOUTHEASTERN WOODLAND DESIGNS
Copyright © 2018 by Cyna's 3E. First Edition Second Printing 2018, Printed and Bound in USA.
All Rights Reserved. You may use the designs and drawings in this book for arts and crafts applications in an educational setting as long as you do not use more than four in any one project or publication. (For permission of any additional use, please contact the author/publisher).

Other Copyright Information: Reproduction or republication of any illustrations and writings for any other project or graphic work in any form or design is strictly prohibited.
Publisher's Address: Cyna's 3E, PO BOX 3719 Pembroke, NC 28372 www.cynas3e.org

SOUTHEASTERN WOODLANDS MAP

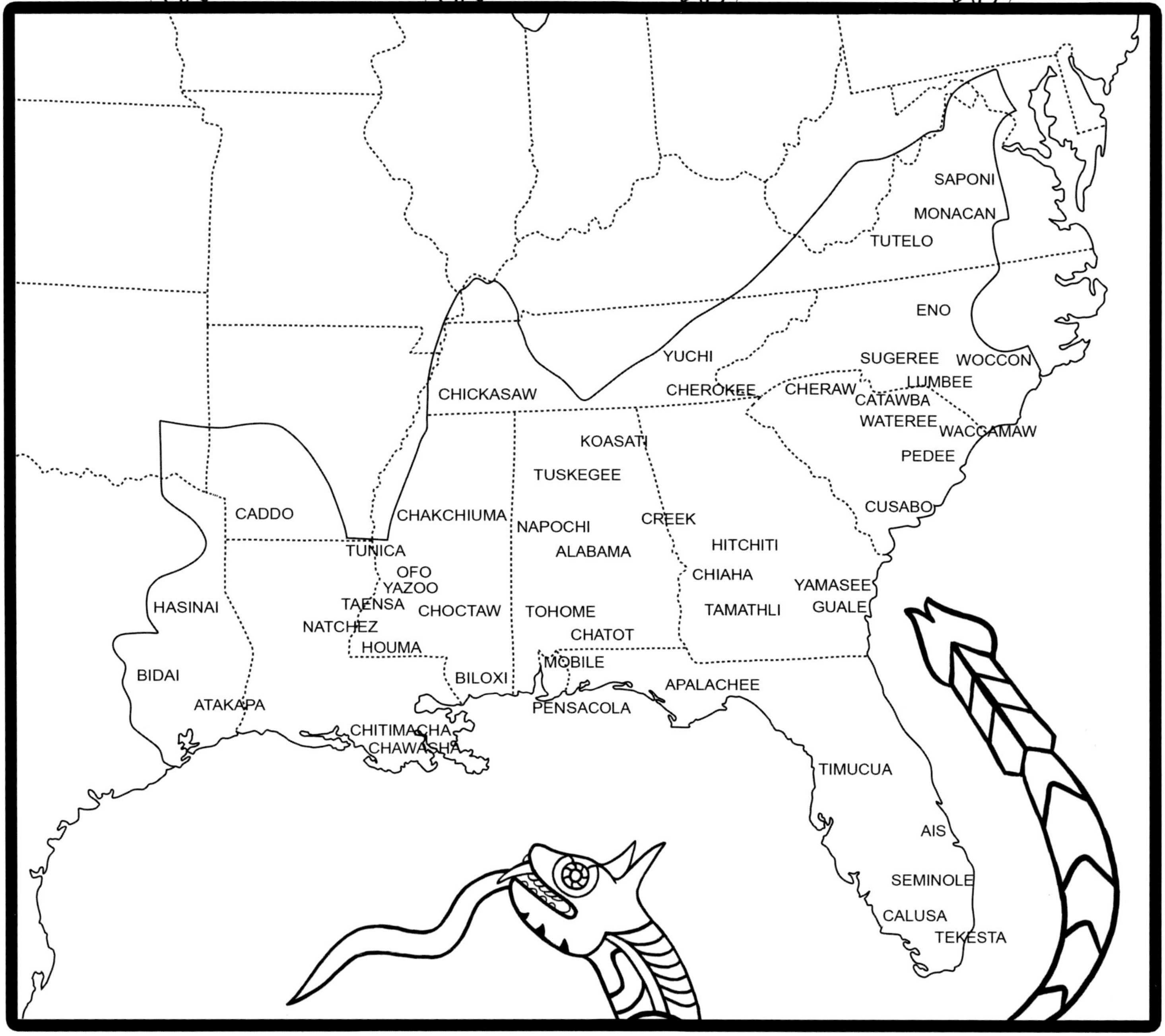

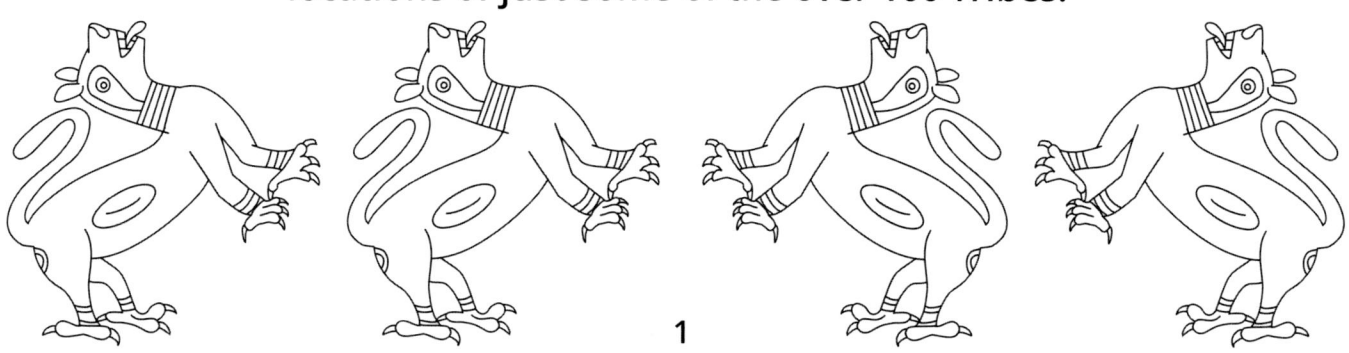

The South East Woodland American Indian Culture area showing approximate locations of just some of the over 100 Tribes.

PINECONE PATCHWORK

Women of the Lumbee Tribe of the past and present stitch these beautiful designs on quilts in their communities. The traditional clothing of Lumbee Women is adorned with the Pinecone Patchwork. This distinct design derives its name from the long leaf pinecone. When looking at the bottom of the pinecone one can find the inspiration for the patchwork design. Special thanks to Miss Kat Littleturtle Clark and Mr. Hayes Alan Locklear of the Lumbee Tribe for reviving this design.

SEVEN SPIRAL SACRED LINES

Among some of the South Eastern Tribes seven was a sacred number. It represented the total number of directions: East, South, West, North, Up, Down and Center. It also represented the number of days in a week. Lines in a spiral pattern indicated no end. The V shape was very common in South Eastern designs and stands for the 7 directions.

BIRDMAN

Of all the birds in the South East the Falcon was the most respected for its ability to fly higher than any other bird and to hunt prey with a powerful blow. The Falcon was also well-regarded for its amazing eye sight. Warriors of South Eastern Tribes often dressed like the Falcon as seen in this picture. The little round circles on his arms, neck, waist and knees are bands of shells or pearls used for adornment.

CAROLINA PANTHERS

Long before the National Football League (NFL) had a team called the Carolina Panthers there were Panthers all over the South East. They ranged from Virginia to Florida. The Panther was so revered that male children were often raised on the skins of the Panther in hopes they would absorb the traits of the Panther such as powerful smelling, fierce strength, cunning thinking and an amazing springing jump.

SOUTHEASTERN MEDICINE WHEEL

This is the South Eastern Medicine Wheel. It was a sign of life and specifically the Circle of Life. The circle symbolizes perfection as well as infinity since the circle has no beginning or end. The over lapping ovals represent the inter-linking of all things in life. There can be many reasons behind the meaning of the circle, the ovals and the dots among the Nations and may signify the following:
The Four Directions: East, South, West, North.
The Four Seasons: Spring, Summer, Autumn, Winter.
The Four Stages of Life: Birth, Youth, Adult, Death.
The Four Times of Day: Sunrise, Noon, Sunset, Midnight.
The Four Elements of Life: Earth, Fire, Water, Wind.
The Four Trials of Man: Success, Defeat, Peace, War.
The Heavenly Beings: Sun, Moon, Earth, Stars.

WATER SPIDER

The Spider was treasured as a clever animal because it could weave and catch prey using stealth and intelligence. The Water Spider was a part of the creation stories of many South Eastern Tribes as the one that gave or brought fire to The People. Water Spider was always referred to as a Female. The circles on her back signifies the bowl she weaved to carry the tiny coal back to The People to start their fires.

CHUNKEY PLAYER

Chunkey was a popular sport played among many of the Tribes of the South East. A round polished stone about the size of a dinner plate was rolled along a prepared playing area. Warriors would then try and throw a special pole that was about 8 feet long at the place where they thought the stone might stop. They did not throw the pole at the stone. Chunkey was more important and more popular than the Stick Ball Game before the arrival of the White Man.

COILED HORNED SERPENT

The coiled horned serpent was believed to help people when they were sick. It was also thought to keep witches away from a person's home. Snake was the character for the warm season of April to October and also for rivers. Many rivers were called Long Snake along with the name of the river.

TURKEY

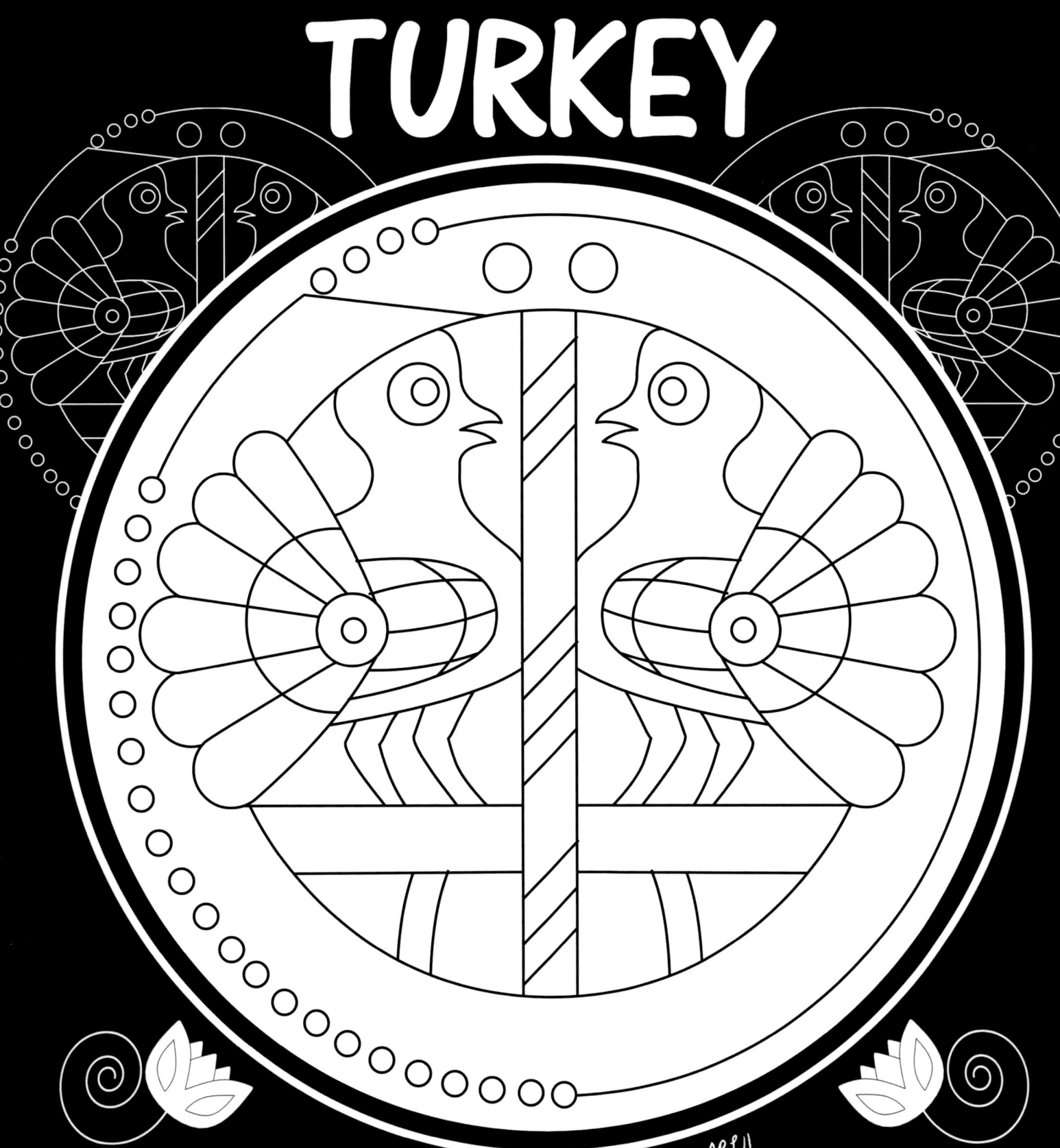

The Wild Turkey was an important bird for the South East Nations. It provided meat for food and much needed feathers that were used for decoration and clothing. The large and extremely durable feathers were used for the fletching on arrows, for bedding, and for clothing such as woven cloaks (a coat like garment) and mantles (a jacket like garment). The Wild Turkey was a large and mighty bird and was well treasured.

BIRDMAN WARRIOR

Birdman is either part Man part Falcon or part Falcon part Man. Birdman symbolized the Warrior of the South East Tribes. He is often drawn with a war club in one hand and a severed head in the other hand to show successful combat in battle.

WOODPECKER

The Woodpecker was very smart in protecting its nest. It would drill holes all around a tree trunk to get the sap in the tree to run down the trunk of the tree. This running of the sap would keep snakes from being able to climb the tree and get to the nest. South East Tribes were amazed at the skill of woodpeckers to penetrate tree trunks to find insects for food.

DANCING FEATHERED SERPENTS

This is the figure of the Four Feathered Serpents dancing around a Medicine Wheel. They were often called *"Skysnakes"* and were symbols of life and the renewal of life to some Tribes who referred to them as the guardians of life and water.

SUN HAND & EYE

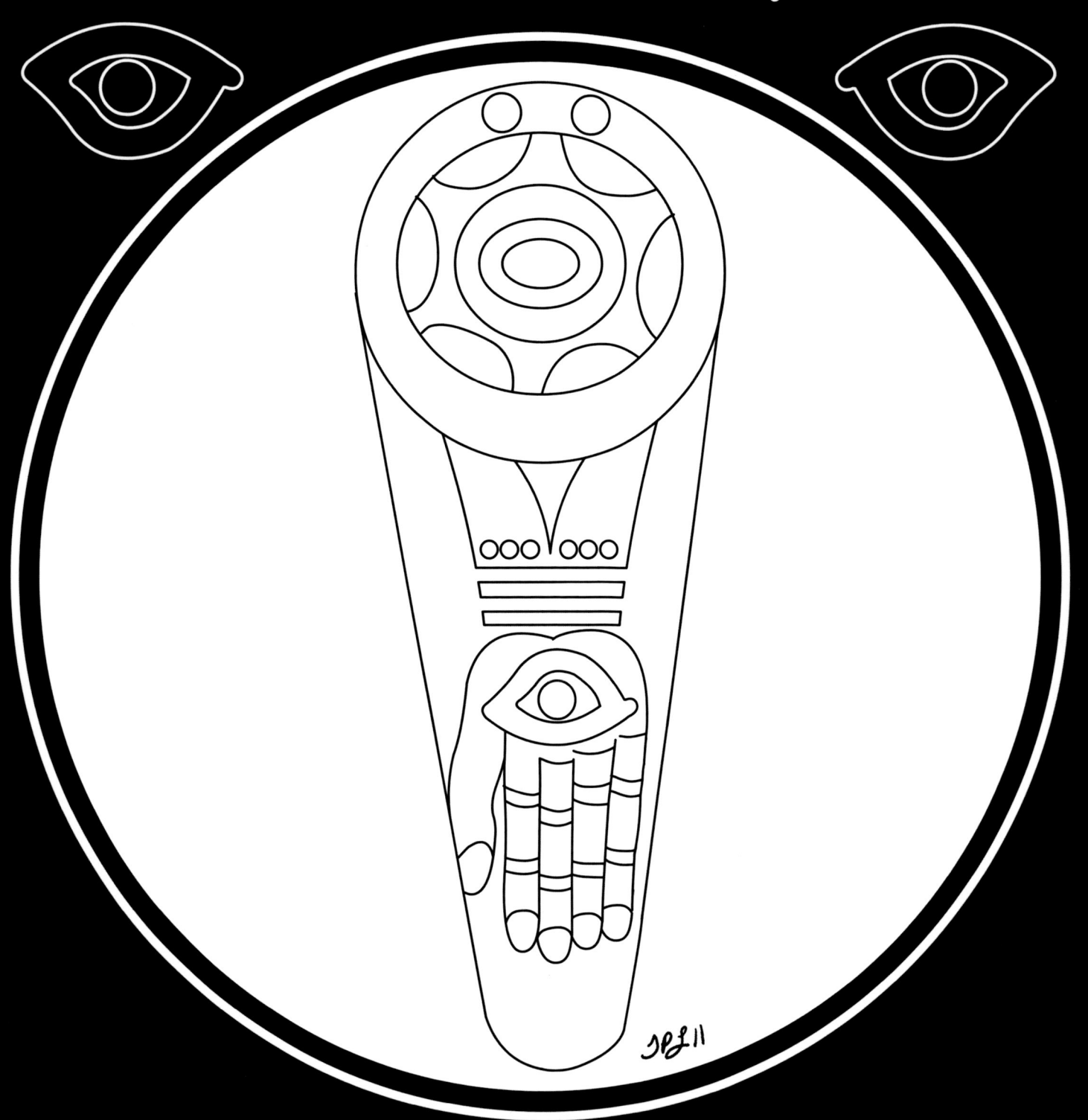

South East Nations felt the Sun was the source of all life and that it watched over all The People. They thought the Sun watched them with a large blazing Eye and as long as the Eye was on them they were protected. When the Sun was not shining or when it was night time Fire took the place of the Sun watching over them. If The People were bad they thought that the Hand of the Sun would punish them.

WOODPECKER II

Woodpecker was swift and cunning and greatly respected by the South East Tribes. Warriors often used Woodpecker feathers for adornment to express this speed and smartness. The call of the Woodpecker was terrifying to many and for this reason the call was often imitated by Warriors to express fear to their enemies.

PANTHER vs FALCON

Contrary to popular belief the Eagle was not the most highly regarded bird of prey among Native Nations of the South East...instead it was the Falcon that was even more admired and honored. The most appreciated animal of prey on land was the Panther. From time to time Panther and Falcon met and had battle to see who was the best Warrior.

DANCING WOODPECKERS

This is the figure of the Four Woodpeckers dancing around the Sun and a Cross. They are dancing the With The Wind direction (or counter-clockwise direction). The Four Woodpeckers and the four continuous lines total the number 8 and were for the Four Directions and the Four Seasons. The Sun has 8 points to also show the Four Directions and Four Seasons.

TURTLE

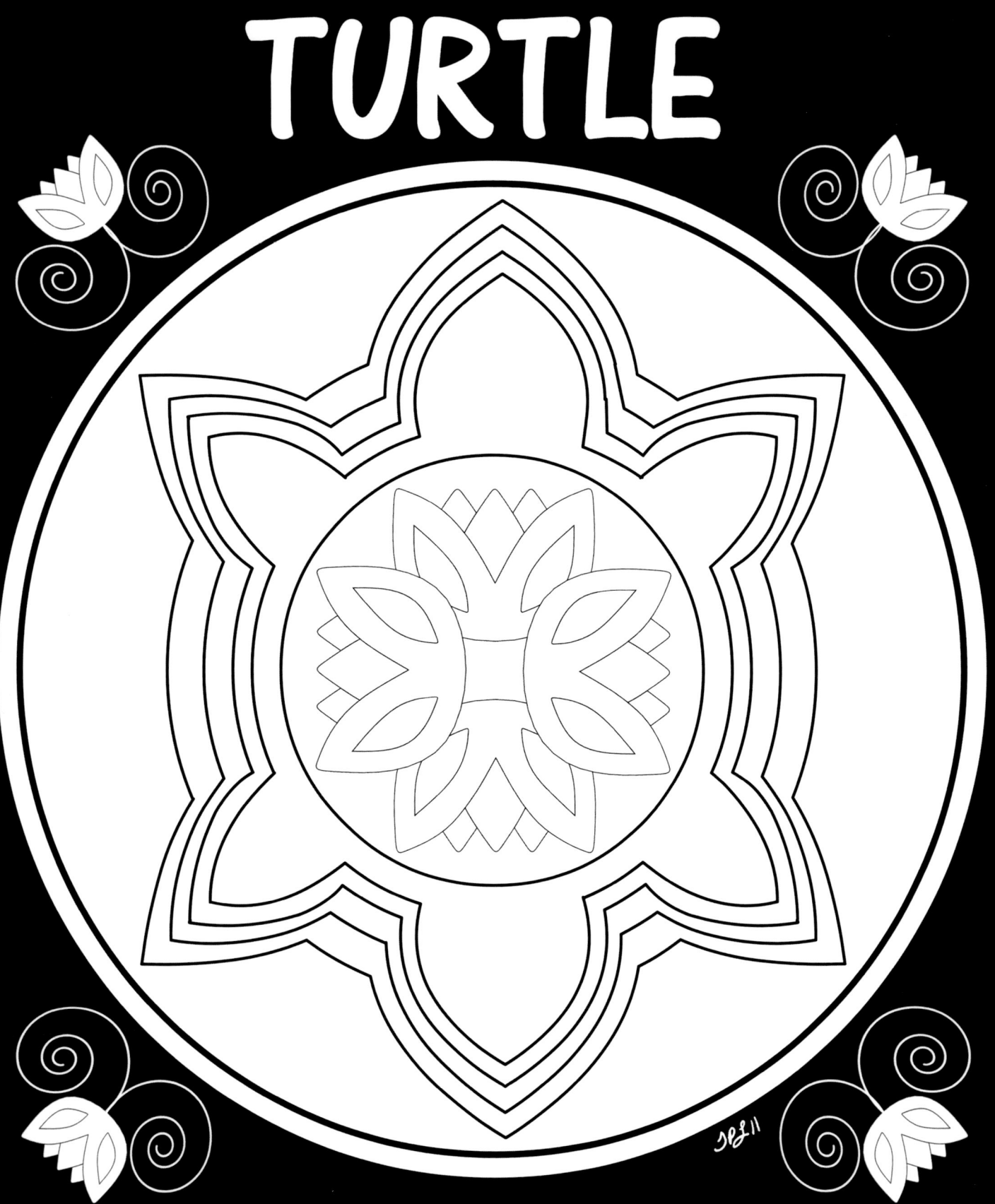

The Turtle in the South East was mainly a source of food and materials. The meat was used in soups and stews and even dried to make jerky. The Turtle was also the main source of eggs for the People. Turtle shells had many uses including containers, bowls, spoons and even shields. Turtle however was a grand image of persistence and patience and its ability to protect itself with its own shell was a particularly valued factor. The famous racing story of the *"Rabbit vs. Turtle"* was really an old South East Native American story and was called *"Turtle Races Deer"* as the Deer was considered the fastest land animal in the South East.

SUN & THUNDER

Among the South East Nations the Sun was considered the source of all life, light and warmth. The Sun was sometimes called *"Ancient White"* and *"Ancient Red"* and *"The Master of Breath."* The representation of the Sun here on Earth was Fire. Thunder was shown by a Bow over the Sun. Thunder was called *"Brother"* and *"Friend"* and was often a source of aid and comfort because He foretold the coming of needed rain.

FEATHERED SERPENT

Peoples of the South East believed in a unique serpent that could fly. Feathered Serpent was also a member of the Rattlesnake family and helped keep witches away from homes. Feathered Serpent could also swim quite well underwater.

SOUTHEAST WARRIOR

This is how a South East Warrior would have dressed around the time period of 1800-1835. Tribes such as the Catawba, Cherokee, Chickasaw, Choctaw, Creek, Seminole, Yuchi and others would have dressed in what was called Long Shirts that came to their knees. They also had center seamed leggings and center seamed moccasins. They used finger woven sashes for belts around their waist and finger woven sashes worn over their shoulders to hold bags or powder horns.

RATTLESNAKES

Of all the snakes in the South East, Rattlesnake was the most feared and the most esteemed. The Rattlesnake was also believed to help keep witches away from the home. These 2 rattlesnakes are circling the all seeing Eye & Hand that was sometimes called *"Bright-Eyed"* or *"Brilliant Looker."* The rattles of the snakes were often used as musical instruments and players of the Ball Game would wear Rattlesnake rattles to make them appear more fearsome. Rattlesnake was called *"Thunder's Necklace"* and the meat was eaten to help prevent diseases and the oil was said to help with arthritis.